BROADWAY SONGS
FOR CLASSICAL PLAYERS

To access recorded piano accompaniments online, visit:
www.halleonard.com/mylibrary

Enter Code
1689-7157-8656-0728

ISBN: 978-1-5400-2267-7

D0584739

Visit Hal Leonard Online at
www.halleonard.com

Contact Us:
Hal Leonard
7777 West Bluemound Road
Milwaukee, WI 53213
Email: info@halleonard.com

In Europe contact:
Hal Leonard Europe Limited
Distribution Centre, Newmarket Road
Bury St Edmunds, Suffolk, IP33 3YB
Email: info@halleonardeurope.com

In Australia contact:
Hal Leonard Australia Pty. Ltd.
4 Lentara Court
Cheltenham, Victoria, 3192 Australia
Email: info@halleonard.com.au

HOW TO USE HAL LEONARD ONLINE AUDIO

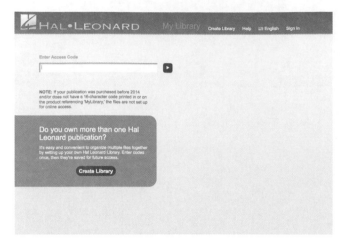

Because of the changing use of media, and the fact that fewer people are using CDs, we have made a shift to companion audio accessible online. In many cases, rather than a book with CD, we now have a book with an access code for online audio, including performances, accompaniments or diction lessons. Each copy of each book has a unique access code. We call this Hal Leonard created system "My Library." It's simple to use.

Go to www.halleonard.com/mylibrary and enter the unique access code found on page one of a relevant book/audio package.

The audio tracks can be streamed or downloaded. If you download the tracks on your computer, you can add the files to a CD or to your digital music library, and use them anywhere without being online. See below for comments about Apple and Android mobile devices.

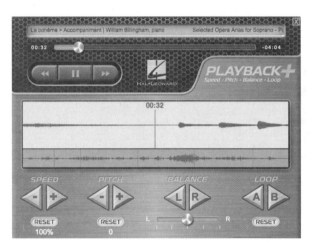

There are some great benefits to the My Library system. *Playback+* is exclusive to Hal Leonard, and when connected to the Internet with this multi-functional audio player you can:

• Change tempo without changing pitch
• Transpose to any key

Optionally, you can create a My Library account, and store all the companion audio you have purchased there. Access your account online at any time, from any device, by logging into your account at www.halleonard.com/mylibrary. Technical help may be found at www.halleonard.com/mylibrary/help/

Apple/iOS

Question: On my iPad and iPhone, the Download links just open another browser tab and play the track. How come this doesn't really download?

Answer: The Safari iOS browser will not allow you to download audio files directly in iTunes or other apps. There are several ways to work around this:

• You can download normally on your desktop computer, saving the files to iTunes. Then, you can sync your iOS device directly to your computer, or sync your iTunes content using an iCloud account.
• There are many third-party apps which allow you to download files from websites into the app's own file manager for easy retrieval and playback.

Android

Files are always downloaded to the same location, which is a folder usually called "Downloads" (this may vary slightly depending on what browser is used (Chrome, Firefox, etc)). Chrome uses a system app called "Downloads" where files can be accessed at any time. Firefox and some other browsers store downloaded files within a "Downloads" folder in the browser itself.

Recently-downloaded files can be accessed from the Notification bar; swiping down will show the downloaded files as a new "card", which you tap on to open. Opening a file depends on what apps are installed on the Android device. Audio files are opened in the device's default audio app. If a file type does not have a default app assigned to it, the Android system alerts the user.

Pianists on the recordings: [1]Brendan Fox, [2]Jamie Johns, [3]Richard Walters

The price of this publication includes access to companion recorded piano accompaniments online,
for download or streaming, using the unique code found on the title page.
Visit **www.halleonard.com/mylibrary** and enter the access code.

All I Ask of You

from *The Phantom of the Opera*

Music by Andrew Lloyd Webber
Lyrics by Charles Hart
Additional Lyrics by Richard Stilgoe

Bring Him Home

from *Les Misérables*

Music by Claude-Michel Schönberg
Lyrics by Herbert Kretzmer and Alain Boublil

If I Loved You

from *Carousel*

Lyrics by Oscar Hammerstein II
Music by Richard Rodgers

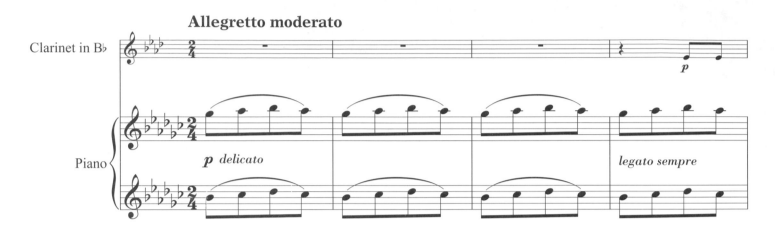

The Impossible Dream
(The Quest)
from *Man of La Mancha*

Lyric by Joe Darion
Music by Mitch Leigh

Pretty Women

from *Sweeney Todd*

Words and Music by
Stephen Sondheim

Languid but steady, non rubato (♩ = 72)

Memory
from *Cats*

Music by Andrew Lloyd Webber
Text by Trevor Nunn after T.S. Eliot

Ol' Man River
from *Show Boat*

Lyrics by Oscar Hammerstein II
Music by Jerome Kern

*The ♪♪ rhythm should more loosely be performed ♪♪ in this section.

Send in the Clowns

from *A Little Night Music*

Words and Music by
Stephen Sondheim

Some Enchanted Evening

from *South Pacific*

Lyrics by Oscar Hammerstein II
Music by Richard Rodgers

The Sound of Music
from *The Sound of Music*

Lyrics by Oscar Hammerstein II
Music by Richard Rodgers

Con espressione

Tonight
(Balcony Scene)
from *West Side Story*

Lyrics by Stephen Sondheim
Music by Leonard Bernstein

Molto meno mosso (sub. in 4)

Adagio (sempre in 4)

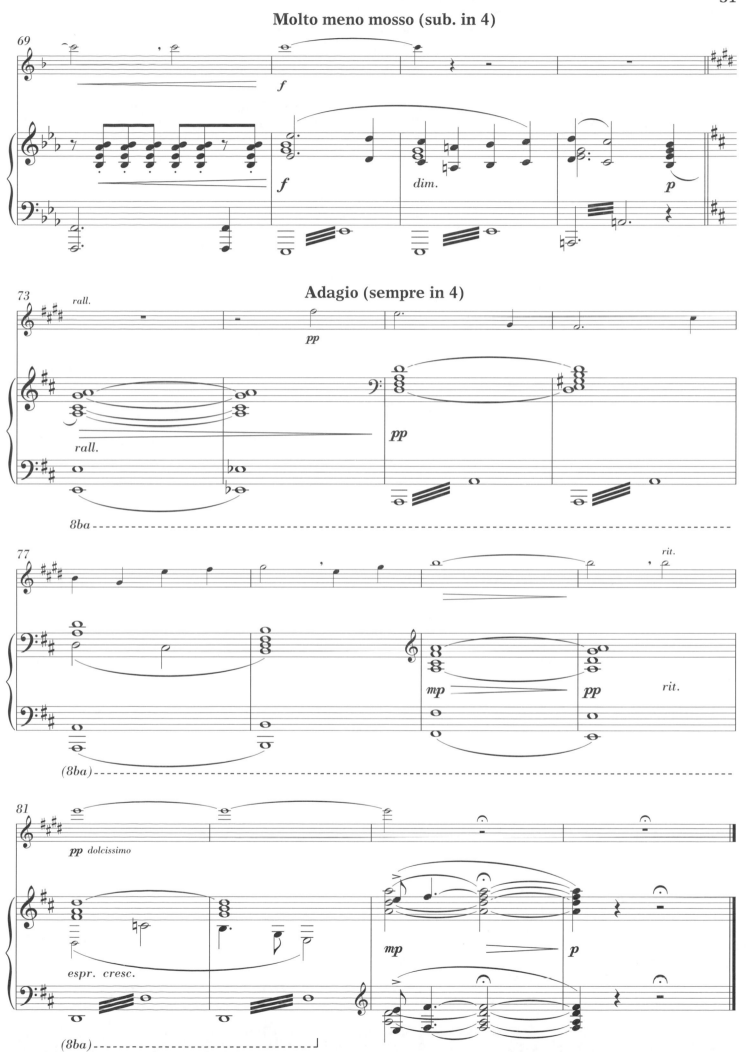

Till There Was You
from Meredith Willson's *The Music Man*

By Meredith Willson